# BIRTH LIKE A MAN

For Amé & Jae

Traditionally, to do things like 'a man' would mean to do something in an overly assertively masculine way. Great if you need to protect your family from an aggressive predator with nothing but a club, but there's no need for assertive masculinity when you're in line for some mediocre beverage at the hospital coffee machine. This book aims to slightly redefine what doing something like a man means in the context of impending parenthood. Because, when people are expecting, the conversation is often about motherhood, fatherhood, or parenthood. Rarely is it about partnerhood. And as you might have guessed, the word 'man' in the title, actually means partner—any partner. But 'Like a Man' just sounded better.

This book is intended for future fathers or non-birthing partners that, like me, think they have a more active, supportive role to play in the delivery of their child than many millennia-old stereotypical gender roles tell you.

In the preparation of that role, I found that many books intended for fathers were very tacky, stereotypical, patriarchal, and not practical enough. So, I figured to write a field guide that is short, snappy, and easily navigable to make being a true parenting partner just a little bit easier.

I sourced my information from books, research, pregnancy classes, family tips, and practical experience, and had it fact-checked by experienced and certified midwives Doriët van Gaalen-Roeleveld and Maxime Welie. Both are awesome.

Doriët is both a mom and a midwife and over the course of her career has seen a lot of different perspectives toward the profession. Having worked in hospital and obstetric practices and having given birth to two beautiful daughters herself, Doriët brought a point of view that I couldn't have done without.

Maxime Welie is an Amsterdam-based midwife who always dreamt of being a doctor but during her studies in the UK and Ghana found her passion for midwifery. Having seen birth in different cultures, she contributed knowledge of great value for creating a book that resonates around the world. She told me that one of the things she has learned from being in people's homes, bedrooms, and delivery rooms is that birth has a way to strip away the trivial and shallow and shows that we all have more in common than we think.

# IN TRO DUC TION

I'm not a gynaecologist,
I'm not a doctor,
I'm not a nurse,
I'm not an assistant,
I'm not an obstetrician,
I'm not a doula,
I'm not a midwife,
I'm not a woman,
Technically you could argue whether or not I'm even a father. At the moment of writing this introduction we have five more weeks to go, three if he's in a hurry. So, I'm definitely not an expert, not even an expert by experience.

I created this book in part to soothe my feelings of unpreparedness, despite all the books and courses. Some sort of idea of support, a life-raft filled with all the things I'm doomed to forget as soon as her water breaks. This also explains its pocket size, or actually its back-pocket size. This book perfectly fits your back pocket, which means it won't get in the way whenever you're being deployed as a human birthing stool or painkiller.

See this book as a beacon of hope whenever you find yourself lost, knee-deep in a birthing-pool with all your clothes still on. Although I'm Dutch, I've packed this book with universal tips, reminders, and summaries, bound by an easy navigation system. So, you should be able to find answers at the turn of a page. I even left some space for your own suggestions or reminders; after all, no baby-delivery is the same.

# CONTENTS

**Before**

**During**



**After**

# WELL BEGUN, HALF DONE

*The importance of the first 1000 days*

Tessa Roseboom, Scientist and Professor of Early Development and Health at the University of Amsterdam, spent 25 years researching how the early environment in which humans grow and develop affects later development and health throughout life. Her findings changed my perspective on pregnancy and early life completely. She captured her research in a book which at this point is only in Dutch, but is a must read if you ask me. The research, though, is in English and is but a Google search away. In a nutshell it proves that, starting at fertilisation, the first 1000 days of a human's life greatly impact their health over the course of their lifetime. She found that what a mother eats during her pregnancy is of far greater influence on the lifespan of a child, than what a child eats after birth. Which means a healthy diet during pregnancy will set your child up for a longer, healthier, and wealthier life.[1]

A lot of a baby's organs develop in the first 12 weeks, and how they do sets the stage for their entire lifetime. For example, the filtering units in your kidneys are formed in Week 30 and these are fixed. You won't be able to make any more units later on in life. If you're born with a low count of filtering units, you'll sooner run into kidney issues then if you'd be born with a great number of them. So, the way you'll be able to cope with kidney challenges at age 30, for example, is truly defined in the first 30 weeks. Tastebuds, food preferences, the ability to cope with stress, heart, or coronary diseases—all these, and many more features are set up in those 1000 days. Well begun is half done.

## WHAT YOU CAN DO



- Read 'The First 1000 Days'. Although the book is only in Dutch at this point, the research isn't. Google 'Effects of Prenatal Exposure to the Dutch Famine on Adult Disease in Later Life: An overview'.[2]
- Watch her TED talk: A Healthier Future by Investing in the best Start in Life | Tessa Roseboom | TEDxAUCollege.[3]
- Support a healthy diet.
- Bring healthy food and snacks like nuts, veggies, fruits, and fish high in Omega-3 fatty acids and low in mercury.
- Help her avoid junk food; however, this can be tricky with certain pregnancy craves.
- Help her avoid stress.
- Help her avoid harmful substances like cigarettes, alcohol, drugs, or any type of harmful food.

KNOW
LEDGE
IS LESS
STRESS

# READ THE FUTURE

*Reading list*

A pregnancy can be intimidating when you don't speak the lingo. Your fragile confidence can be easily shattered when you get bombarded with words like colostrum, oxytocin, Apgar score, sweeping membranes, meconium, or episiotomy. Nineteenth century bacteriologist Louis Pasteur once said, 'chance favours the prepared mind', and for dads it's no different. Invite luck into your world and get prepared. You can do so in many different ways, from changing your nephew's diapers to taking dad-courses and pregnancy evening classes, watching YouTube videos, reading magazines and books, or seeking ye olde lore. Find a way that works for you. Anything goes as long as it educates you on what's to come. The more knowledge you've acquired the easier it will be to dissect wanted, and unwanted, advice and to decide what you'll take on and what you won't. And believe me, if there's one thing you'll get more of than you need, it will be advice.

## WHAT YOU CAN DO

- Read the book 'The First 1000 Days' or the related paper by Tessa Roseboom.[1]
- Read 'The Positive Birth Book' by Milli Hill.[4]
- Find a dad-class nearby.
- Join a pregnancy class with your partner.
- Get 'The Wonder Weeks' book and app (helped me out many times).
- Read this book.
- Watch positive birth movies on YouTube and you'll see that giving birth is less gory than you thought.

# GROWING

*From poppyseed to pumpkin*

In Randall Munroe's book 'What If', he calculated that if a human would keep up the growth pace that a baby experiences in its first month, it would be a 2.08 meters (6'10") tall toddler by age three, 4.2 meters at age seven, and a good ten meters by the time it's twenty.[5] You don't have to worry about a two-meter toddler, but they will grow f-a-s-t. They will grow from a poppyseed to pumpkin between fertilisation and delivery. And after that, they grow even faster. However, babies don't grow linearly. The stats show that your child might grow four centimetres in the first month, but this doesn't happen gradually every day. It can literally be in 48 hours, and that can cause some discomfort for your child.

Besides the physical growth, the mental growth is even more impressive. This happens in something called leaps. There are ten leaps, and each leap unlocks a new set of skills, the child unlocking a new level of comprehension. Some of these new skills can feel scary to your child, as if everything they've just gotten used to has completely changed. So, it's no surprise that each of the leaps can come with crying, neediness, moodiness, or bad sleeping and eating. In books like 'The Wonder Weeks', you can learn what each leap entails and when you can expect what. Knowing what's to come makes it easier to cope with the change and even help you play into it. Just how running ten kilometres with no finish line can be psychologically tougher than running a 20k with a finish line, so too are leaps for a child. Spot the milestones so you can stay sane and get the most out of your mileage.

# WHAT YOU CAN DO



- Get yourself a copy of 'The Wonder Weeks', with accompanying app.
- Become familiar with the baby's growth process in uterus and stimulate their senses by, for example, talking to the belly or playing classical music.
- Stimulate their new-found skills through play. For example, my son loved 'The Baby Art Gallery' and other high-contrast cards during Leap 1 when he could see contrasts, and peek-a-boo during Leap 5 when he understood relationships.
- Dose how you give toys based on their skills. You'll get lots of toys from family and friends. To not over stimulate, dose them at the right time in line with their development.

# HORMONE HOUSEKEEPING

*Embrace the change*

Change is inherent to a pregnancy. Bodies, homes, whole futures change, but before any of that change becomes visible, there is the invisible change that can be very impactful and arrive sooner than you might expect: Hormones. In order to prepare the female body to develop, deliver, and sustain a small human, the body produces HCG (Human Chorionic Gonadotropin), also known as the pregnancy hormone. A beautiful product of nature's engineering, it enables us to detect a pregnancy and it sustains the growth of the embryo. Without it, the body would reject the pregnancy. Besides HCG there are many other hormones in play that can also mean a significant alteration in your partner's behaviour. They'll sleep poorly or wake up early. Some suddenly get an extremely short fuse, flying off the handle over the smallest thing. Others become hopelessly emotional, get an overpowering urge to nest or clean, or get weird cravings. Whether your partner temporarily changes into a demon or an angel, know that they can't do anything about this. All you can do is accept it and support her in this hormonal rollercoaster. One thing you should especially not do is say 'I'm sure it's the hormones' whenever she's being unreasonable, nor get into arguments. There is only loss at the end of those paths. And no-one likes to be a loser.

# WHAT YOU CAN DO

- Accept instead of argue.
- Embrace the change.
- Help soothe the hormones by reducing stress.
- Help her settle pregnancy craves.
- Hormones can sometimes have her crave plaster, dry-wall, or chalk—a condition called pica that results from an iron deficiency. If she does, consult a doctor or midwife.
- Support any urge to nest or clean. Remodel the house. Fix things you've put off for months. Get out a mop and bucket. You know the drill.

# EATING BACKWARDS

*Nausea and morning sickness*

After seeing the plus sign on your pregnancy test there are a lot of positives to cheer for, but also some negatives. Morning sickness or pregnancy nausea can be one. Not all women have to deal with it, but for those who do, it can be a pain. Despite of all the brilliant people we have in the world it still hasn't been conclusively proven what causes it, though it is strongly believed to be related to hormonal changes, specifically, the pregnancy hormone HCG, or Human Chorionic Gonadotropin, responsible for setting up the pregnancy for success. The actual HCG values cannot be influenced, the nausea or morning sickness, however, can be. From her eating smaller bites more often throughout the day to taking ginger pills, there's a lot to try out when it comes to making her pregnancy more bearable, and let's be honest, your life as well.

## WHAT YOU CAN DO



- Invite her to eat lighter snacks more often throughout the day, from the moment she wakes to when she goes to bed. Bring her some fibre crackers, small vegetable snacks, or yoghurt.
- Eating before she gets up in the morning also helps, so leave some light crackers on her bedside table.
- Log her nausea triggers on your fridge or phone notes to remind yourself what not to make or bring her.
- Get her some ginger pills.
- Eating and drinking sour things like citrus fruits or diluted apple vinegar can help.
- Chewing gum and peppermint can also help
- Make her ginger tea.
- Sometimes the force of the hormones is just too strong, in which case you should just make sure she drinks a lot of water and make sure she has a hair band. Nobody's looking forward to brushing vomit out of a new haircut.
- Give her a glass of water to rinse her mouth afterwards so the acids won't harm the enamel of her teeth. Mix a bit of baking soda with water to neutralise the acids if you have the time.
- Alternative medicines have often proven helpful; consider booking an appointment at an acupuncturist, acupressurist, or book an aromatherapy session.
- If the nausea is unbearable and nothing helps, reach out to your doctor to get some medicine to suppress it. In some cases, the nausea can get so bad that she won't be able to keep anything down throughout the day. In such cases hospitalisation might be required to guarantee the safety of mother and child.

# DON'T REVEAL THE NAME

# NAMING THEM

*Giving them a name before they have one*



I never quite got the whole problem with sharing a baby's name before it is born, until my partner pointed out a story to me. There was a woman who was simultaneously pregnant with her sister and she shared the names she had dreamt about naming her kids. Her sister delivered her baby first and used both of her sisters 'dream-names' to name her newborn. Two of her ideal names, for one child. Total. Dick. Move. And a good reason to work with a placeholder name. Because sisters can't steal what they don't know exists. If you use the actual name while being pregnant, chances are that you're going to reveal it unintentionally at some point. In my case, twice. Luckily, no one realised. You wouldn't be the first blabbing out your future baby's name before it's actually delivered, but you might very well be the last depending on how attached your partner was to that name. Another benefit of using a placeholder name is that you can have fun with what you call them until then. Nacho, Minion, Mister Potato-head, mini-me, or if you're feeling more ironic, 'the accident'.

## WHAT YOU CAN DO

- Do not reveal the real name prematurely.
- Do not reveal the real name prematurely.
- Do not reveal the real name prematurely.
- Do not reveal the real name prematurely.
- Do not reveal the real name prematurely.
- Come-up with placeholder names.

# ANNOUNCING THE NEWS

*Announcing the good news*

One of the first questions that pops up when you see that positive test is 'when are we going to announce it'. The unwritten rule is to announce after 12 weeks, which partly stems from the fear of having to talk about a potential miscarriage if you tell sooner. And although the chances of a miscarriage are real—9-15% if your partner is younger than 35, 20% between 35 and 40, and it increases form there[6] —it is weird there's still such a taboo on something so common. Forcing women and partners to keep this emotional burden to themselves isn't right, especially when you realise that being able to talk about it with friends and families helps in the healing and grieving process.[7] It should be up to themselves to be able to talk about it or not and shouldn't be dictated by some dated taboo.[8]

The reason that the 12-week mark exist is because of the 12-week scan. Generally speaking, this is the first big milestone, and the period leading up to the scan has the highest risk of bad news. During this ultrasound they'll confirm the due date and check the overall health of your unborn prodigy and whether or not you'll be getting two for the price of one. Depending on the country of residence they might invite you to do a NIPT test, which is basically bloodwork and DNA sequencing to spot things like Down (trisomy 21), Edward's (trisomy 18), and Patau's (trisomy 13) syndrome or additional chromosomal disorders. The first one I'm sure you're already familiar with. I won't go into detail about the other two, but even though they're much rarer than Down syndrome they're almost always fatal. Hence the check.

There are a lot of ethical questions on whether or not you should or should not check for these kinds of things, but ultimately, it's up to you. Being the control freak that I am, I wanted to be prepared for whatever was coming to make sure our baby had a soft landing onto this planet.



## WHAT YOU CAN DO

- Discuss with your partner an announcement plan. How do you want to share with parents, family, and friends?
- Devise a vision of how much you want or don't want to know during the pregnancy.
- Discuss whether or not you want to do a NIPT test.
- If you are unsure and need consultation, reach out to your doctor or midwife.

# GENDER REVEAL

*The event of revealing the gender*

There are few surprises left in life, and although I'd always thought we'd keep the gender of our child a mystery until we could see it with our own eyes, as soon as the sonographer asked us if we wanted to know, curiosity got the better of us. No confetti or cake for our gender reveal party, but just the sonographer telling us what the gender was going to be. Exactly how we liked it; a moment we wanted to keep to ourselves.

If you do want a good excuse for a party, plan a gender reveal party. At the 20-week ultrasound ask the sonographer to write the gender on a piece of paper and seal it in an envelope. If you want to be surprised as well, ask a friend to plan the party with you. Depending on your partner, making it a surprise to her can be a welcome move. If not, make sure she's involved. Don't plan your date until you've gotten the gender confirmation from your sonographer, sometimes they might need you to come back because the baby sits at a funny angle. But once you know. Plan away.

There are some practical advantages to consider when you decide to keep it a mystery or not, like having more guidance on what clothes to buy and nursery to put together and reading up on boys versus girls. The irony is that in our case we picked a gender-neutral name, nursery, and wardrobe so none of the advance knowledge was actually beneficial to us.

# WHAT YOU CAN DO

- Ask your partner what she would like to do when it comes to revealing gender.
- Plan the 20-week ultrasound. The ideal moment for this check-up is between week 19 and 20. They can already tell the gender from week 16 onwards so if you're impatient you might be able to organise a 'fun ultrasound' specifically for this purpose.
- Ask the sonographer to write the gender down and seal it.
- Get a friend or family member involved in the planning.
- Come up with reveal ideas: cake, piñata, balloon pop, confetti, burnouts, baseballs, paintballs...you name it, but keep it sane. There have been plane crashes, blown-up houses, and even deceased family members due to 'original' reveals. Nothing worse than killing grandpa by announcing his grandson or daughter, so stay safe out there.

# BONDING STARTS IN HER BELLY

# PRE-BONDING

*The beginning of your relationship with your child*



Besides the discomforts that come with having a baby in her belly, there are many advantages that your partner will experience: always a seat in public transport, smiling faces wherever she goes, but one of the most important is baby bonding. From the moment of conception, your partner will build a bond with your baby. They share food, emotions, even oxygen, and over time the baby will hear her heartbeat, voice, and laugh. So, it's no surprise that mothers have a head start in bonding with your baby. However, your bonding moment opportunities start sooner than you think. After about 18 weeks[9] your baby will be able to hear voices, barking, and even music outside of the womb—the perfect moment to introduce them to your voice. It might feel silly at first but talking to the belly multiple times a day will create a sense of familiarity around your voice. So, make a ritual of talking to the belly when you get up and before you go to bed, you'll be surprised to see that in time they will start to respond. I've had many times that when I had my head on her belly and was talking that I got a 'kick-to-the-head'.

## WHAT YOU CAN DO

- Talk to the belly starting at week 20.
- Start your baby's musical education from week 20 onwards.
- Sing songs, any song. if you want to bust out Ice Cube's 'It Was a Good Day' do it.

*Choosing your birthing partner*

Some things in life require a professional. Like redoing your electrical work, plumbing, or moving walls. Delivering a baby, is definitely on the list of 'don't try this alone'. Although the human body is built to reproduce, and hypothetically you don't per se need anyone to deliver a baby, it is wise to find a professional to guide your process. The art of obstetrics requires a wealth of knowledge and experience that should be instantly available. The knowledge you've gained from podcasts, classes, books, and consults vanish into thin air when the big moment finally arrives and the last thing you want is to have to make decision based on how fast your sweaty sausage fingers can type 'how to prevent perineal tears'. A midwife is faster than your word-type-count and less stressful for you, be it a midwife that is in line with the birth vision you and your partner have. This is also the starting point of finding the right midwife; choose one that fits your personal values and shares your pregnancy vision. Defining that vision is important, should the baby be delivered in the hospital or at home? Naturally or medically? Do you want a midwife? A doula? A relative? Birthing is choosing, so make sure you choose well informed.

# WHAT YOU CAN DO



- Discuss the core values of the delivery.
- Discuss the birthing partner preferences. E.g. doula, midwife, relative or doctor.
- Ask friends and family for their experiences.
- Look for midwives and research their values so you can find one with shared values.
- Look for a midwife nearby as your partner will visit them often.
- Assume the worst-case scenario and then ask yourself if this midwife will be able to guide you through.
- Check if the midwife is covered by your insurance.

# CHANGE OF BIRTH PLAN

*Creating your birth plan*

This will probably be one of the few life plans you make that will go up in flames as soon as the first waves of contractions begin, which is okay. The primary purpose of a birth plan is to get a clear picture of what your partner and you do and don't want during labour. Some want a natural birth in the middle of a creek and others will want to be completely sedated. Whatever your preferences, it needs a bit of preparation and that is what a birth plan is for. It ensures you've thought about the many different scenarios and outcomes and have an opinion or idea about what may arise. You might not have time to ponder a decision like sweeping the membranes or breaking the water in the heat of the moment, so knowing how a decision will affect the process in advance and having an opinion about it helps. It will also help to get midwives, doulas, or gynaecologist on board with your plan. A birth plan will enable you to make decisions whenever your partner is unable to do so without risking resentment afterwards. On the next page you'll find a few things to consider.

# WHAT YOU CAN DO



- Set up the outline of a birth plan; key questions to answer:

- **Plan**
  What is your ideal scenario and when is it okay to deviate from it? Where does she want to give labour? What space? Does she want to be involved in decisions about her and the baby, and if so, which ones? Does she mind cervix dilation checks? Is there any trauma to consider?

- **People**
  Who does she want in the room? Who represents her interests should she not be able to?

- **Pain**
  Does she want painkillers? If so, which and when? Are there specific interventions she doesn't want? What are her preferences should a C-section be needed?

- **Positions**
  List ideal position options.

- **Post-natal**
  Who catches the baby? Who cuts the umbilical cord? Where should the tests on the baby be performed? What should happen to the placenta? If she can't hold the baby herself, who should? Formula or breastfeeding?

- Print your birth plan a couple of times and put it in your go-bag .

# ACKNOWLEDGING THE BABY

*Acknowledgement of parentage*

Whenever you find your partner pregnant out of wedlock you basically have two options. Put a ring on it and tie the knot or raise your child as a 'bastard' and live like heathens. Immersing yourself into the institution of marriage or remaining a free spirit are equally beautiful for different reasons. However, when it comes to raising a child there are some benefits to being married opposed to not. In short, being married means you automatically have parental responsibility whereas when you are not married, you don't. You will need to acknowledge your baby and register as the father. In a lot of cases this should happen within a few days after birth but in my country you can already do this before the child is born. Each country has different legislation, so if the institution of marriage is not for you, be sure to inform yourself about your obligations when it comes to acknowledging your child. Your parenthood and legal dad-ness are depending on it.

Another thing that often falls onto the shoulders of the non-birthing partner is registering your child with the government. In most cases it's a matter of submitting information like name, date of birth, sex, and some other details. It's kind of important to get this right because this is what makes your child exist legally. Don't screw up the name. Write it down with your partner to make sure you're both thinking the same thing when it comes to spelling. The last thing you want is having your dyslexia scar your child for life.

# WHAT YOU CAN DO

- Discuss with your partner what kind of union feels right for you both.
- Learn about the union options available in your country.
- Learn about your responsibilities and rights as a non-birthing partner.
- Acknowledge your parenthood in time.
- Register your child with the government.
- Align with your partner as to the spelling of your child's name.
- Register your child in time and with the right details.

# A PENNY SAVED A PENNY EARNED

# MONEY





*Babies cost money*

The impending bill that comes with a pregnancy can leave many non-birthing partners with sweaty palms, so it's no surprise many start to worry about money or become more interested in making it. Cost can significantly differ based on the country where you're raising your child. In my case almost all cost of delivering a child is covered by my insurance and state. But it's always good to make sure you have some savings lined up should you be confronted with unexpected cost.
When it comes to the baby trousseau, you'll have plenty of options to be smart with your expenses. Some of the things that are branded essential aren't. For example, you can buy a co-sleeper. But because you will only use it six months, it can be more economic and sustainable to borrow, rent, or buy one second hand. For each of the big expenses there are alternatives. So, make sure you have a point of view on what you want to have brand new and what you don't, because a child will be expensive and all the expenses you can save will find a way to be spent elsewhere.

## WHAT YOU CAN DO

- Decide on what crib you want brand new, second hand, or rented.
- Make an inventory of things that sit idle in the basements and attics of friends and families and learn what you could potentially utilise.
- Basic clothing like bodysuits or pyjamas can easily be bought second hand. They grow so fast that most of the things offered second hand have been worn very few times.
- Think about generating passive income; royalties through writing a book, music, podcasts, or invest in ETF's or stock, real estate, or any kind of intellectual property. Find investments that suit you.
- Read books on financial literacy.
- Start saving up and investing in the name of your child.

# NURSERY

*What is needed in a nursery*

There are many things a non-birthing parent simply can't do, but the nursery is most definitely one with which you can lead the charge. However, you can silence that little panicky voice in the back of your head that keeps on shouting that you really need to start getting the nursery together, because for the first six months your baby will probably be sleeping in your bedroom. This differs per parent of course, but most of the time they'll be in a co-sleeper next to the bed so it's easy to comfort or breastfeed without having to get out of bed. The only reason you want to have the nursery ready before birth is that once your little one has arrived, you won't have the energy or time to fix it all. But relax, you have nine months to get this thing in order, which should be more than enough.

# WHAT YOU CAN DO



- Treat the wall next to your nursery dresser with a water-repelling agent, so potential diaper stains come out of your wall with a simple wipe.
- Get a mobile (silicone) night light so whenever you're on your own and need to walk around the house, you don't have to wake up your baby with all the bright house lights. It's also a great light source when changing diapers at night and (depending on your light) can double as a fun light toy for your baby.
- Any drawer cabinet can work as a nursery dresser and might cost less and look better; just make sure it's wide enough.
- Get a nursery dresser with drawers so you don't have to fumble around with cabinets.
- Get drawer dividers and categorise by item. Everything you use most goes in the top drawer. Then work your way down in order of relevance.
- Avoid too much stuff on your dresser because your baby will get hold of it all.
- Get multiple change pad covers.
- Avoid things on the wall they can pull down or that can come down.

# CAR SEAT

*Navigating the car seat world*

Having, in advance, a car seat is essential to any parent, even more so if your baby will be delivered in the hospital because most hospitals won't let you leave if you don't have a car seat. Even if you live within walking distance of a hospital, don't expect that your partner, baby, and you will be strolling back under a romantic moon. So, unless you're planning on living at the hospital until they're a teen, get a car seat. Besides being able to leave the hospital, there's another great perk; it reduces the risk of death for children under age one by 71%[10] and reduces the risk of hospitalisation by 67% for children age four and under.[11] Nothing like the threat of death to convince you into a purchase.

Now that you're convinced, getting the right one is easier said than done. There are so many options available that it can be overwhelming finding the one for you. Size, weight, isofix or seatbelt, legroom, side impact protection—all important aspects of picking the right one. And although there are many things you can definitely get second hand, unless you know the exact history of a car seat because it belonged to a friend or relative, I'd strongly advise against getting it second hand. Like a motorcycle helmet, it's very difficult to see from the outside whether or not it has structural damage. So be sure, or get it brand new.

# WHAT YOU CAN DO



- Make sure the car seat is certified.
- When buying a baby car seat with isofix, already take the follow-up, toddler child seat into consideration when choosing. Isofix base-plates aren't universal, so unless you want some extra cost, make sure you have an isofix that is compatible with multiple seats.
- The centre of the backseat is the safest place to install a car seat since the centre doesn't take direct impact.[12]
- If you don't have a middle seat, then the backseat behind the passenger seat is the second safest place in the car because this is the furthest away from the opposing traffic side, and unloading is easier.[12]
- Always install a baby car seat facing the rear. When children are older they can face the front.
- Make sure it has side impact protection. Cars don't have crumple zones to the sides, and with your kid sitting higher in the car, they're less protected by the steel in the car, making them more vulnerable in potential side collisions.
- Make sure it's easy to install, so there is little room for error.
- As soon as you have it, install it in your car, you don't want to figure this out when you should be driving to the hospital.

# DAY CARE

*Figuring out your support system*

That pink cloud, beautiful as it can be, will eventually evaporate and when it does you want to make sure you have your support system for when you go back to work figured out. Whether one of you will stay at home and care for your little one, or if the grandparents, brother, sister, or cousin take a few days a week, or if you'll bring them to day care, you better start early with making plans. There will be a lot on both of your minds, and this is one you can check off your list early. Just one less thing to worry about when you're mastering parenthood.

Depending on where you live, day cares can have long waiting lists, so enquire in your area about the wait. In my case, we registered with three day cares at week 15, which was considered late. If your family pitches in, it's best to start that conversation early as well, so everyone can prepare for the new responsibility, nay... privilege, of caring for your newborn.

## WHAT YOU CAN DO

- Devise a point of view on what you both think is important in the care of your child and make a plan accordingly. Think of food, stimulation/ play, sleep, socialisation, exploration, and disciplining.

**Family care**

- Make clear arrangements and discuss your preferences. Think about rhythms, feeding styles, boundaries, or disciplinary styles.
- With family, discuss how you'll handle care cost.
- Put a reminder in your calendar once a month to bring a little appreciative gift. This will go a long way.
- Accept differences in caring styles as no one will do it like you would.

**Day care**

- When selecting day care, define questions based on your point of view to ask staff:
- Key questions:
  - How long have you been in business?
  - Are you licensed?
  - What kind of accreditations do you have?
  - What are the pick-up and drop-off times, and how flexible are these?
  - What is your policy when a baby is ill?
  - What meals are provided, and what do those consist of?
  - Are diapers supplied and what kind? (Are they biodegradable? Do they accept cloth diapers?)
  - How are the children grouped? Horizontal (mixed age) or vertical (by age)?
  - How diverse is the staff/baby group?
  - What is the child-to-staff ratio?
  - Do you have a parent portal or app that shares live updates?
- Most day care chains will have multiple locations, and a hack to guarantee a spot is to let them know you're open to take any location in your area. Once you're registered with a location that maybe isn't the one you were hoping for, let them know you prefer another location and you'll be placed on the internal waiting list. Internal waiting lists have priority to the public ones.
- When you have the day care interview make sure to align with them on your baby's sleeping patterns, pacifier preferences, baby comforter, food.

# BABY SHOWER

*Hers, not yours*

To celebrate the arrival of the impending offspring and to help the parents prepare in the last few weeks, there is the baby shower. A surprise-party-like event where friends and family bring gifts, play games, have snacks, and above all, put the mom-to-be in the spotlight. Nowadays, baby showers aren't restricted to moms alone; very poorly named 'Manshowers' or 'Dadchelors' are popping up all over the place. A celebration of you transforming from a man into a dad. From having to rap baby-books to eating disgusting baby vegetable jars it feels more like a hazing than a party, but often there's beer, so it's not all bad. However, this chapter is about how you can support the baby shower of your partner. Often it is organised by a friend or sibling, but still relies on your support. If you're unaware if something is being organised, inquire with her friends. A reason might be that you're also invited and therefore kept in the dark. If nothing is being organised, try to cast a baby shower planner. Baby showers can be a nice moment of relief and distraction in those last weeks and it would be a shame if the opportunity passes. Unless your partner hates these kinds of things. Then let it pass. Obviously.

## WHAT YOU CAN DO



- Discuss your partner's wishes regarding a baby shower.
- Ask around if something is being organised. If not, cast a party planner.
- Share the wishes of your partner with the party planner.
- Create a list or registry of things you and your partner still need.
- Support in organising the surprise.
- On the day of the baby shower, come up with an excuse for her to dress up a bit. Letting her rock up in her jammies might not be forgiven easily.
- Find out if you're welcome at the shower or not., iIf not, stay away.

# BABYMOON

*The last trip...for a while*

Babymoon. I did not come up with this term. It is a real thing. Like a honeymoon, it is a celebratory vacation but contrary to a honeymoon this happens before the big moment, in the second trimester to be precise. The biggest side effects of starting up the pregnancy, like morning sickness and the lack of energy, are mostly gone, the belly isn't big enough to be an obstacle, and it's often a trimester filled with energy. It's a perfect time to enjoy some adventure before the weight of the end of term and the obligations of parenthood appearing on the horizon. Some airlines don't accept pregnant passengers after 36 weeks, so make sure to check with the airline or avoid going too late in the pregnancy.

The idea behind a babymoon is to take little breather together before the adventure of birth begins and to have your last trip with only the two of you. It might also be a while before you're comfortable enough to travel with your baby again, and even when you do, it won't be the same. Travel with a third will still be great, but different. So even if it's just a long weekend one hour away, do it, you'll remember it forever.

# WHAT YOU CAN DO



- Avoid long travel times.
- Avoid Zika-affected destinations, and if you do make sure you are both using bug repellent because Zika can also be transmitted sexually.[13]
- Plan for the second trimester, or around for to five months.
- Bring a pregnancy pillow.
- Keep in mind that pregnant women have a higher body temperature and that extremely hot destinations might not be comfortable for her.
- Keep the local cuisine in mind when picking a destination as you don't want her to get nauseous at every turn of a corner.
- She can snowboard or ski up to twelve weeks safely (depending on her skills). After that, consult a midwife or doctor before you leave.
- Avoid destinations above 2150m (7053ft) during the entire pregnancy. High altitudes reduce the amount of oxygen in the blood, which can harm mother and child.

# BIRTH CARD

*The card of cards*

You could argue that it's strange we still send letters or cards in this day and age, but there's something about a social post or a group chat announcement that doesn't do justice to the majestic arrival of your offspring, efficient as it may be. So, make sure you have everything sorted for your birth card a few weeks in advance. First think about whether you want to have something custom designed or if you'll utilise the vast catalogues of printers out there. If it's the latter you can basically just order it in the days after birth, easy-peasy. If you're working with a custom design, you'll need to start a few months in advance. Find the artists you'd like to design the card, discuss style, paper, envelope, inspiration, rates, and deadline. Most of the time they'll know a good printer as well but otherwise you can get the designer to give you the print-files and you can sort it yourself. Make sure that everything is ready to go and all it needs is an update on birthdate, weight, and size. When it comes to your address list, keep it simple and create a Google Form that anyone can fill out so you can collect the addresses you need and have them all instantly in a single file. All you have to do is share the link. This can also be a convenient way to get addresses of your distant cousins as your parents or aunts and uncles can share the link with them as well. Even if your card isn't printed yet, you can already get your envelopes so you can prep these in advance with stamps and address stickers. With some one-stop-shop baby card printers you can even give them the list and they'll print and post for you—a convenient solution when you'd rather fall asleep than fold cards.

## WHAT YOU CAN DO

- Create a Google Form to collect addresses.
- Collect examples of cards you like.
- Align on the approach for the cards.
- Find an artist or designer you'd like to design it.
- Find a one-stop-shop printer.
- Order paper samples in advance.
- Stamp and address envelopes in advance.

# BIRTH PHOTOGRAPHER

*Family in the making photos*

Ask any woman about her delivery and you're likely to hear how they can't remember all of the details. A beautiful feature of the human body and mind that ensures that mothers still consider another child after birth. It's also partly the reason of a new rising industry, that of the birth photographer: a professional that is skilled in taking photos and videos in the delivery room without distracting the mom-to-be, caregivers, and yourself. You will both be so engaged with the delivery that finding a moment to snap a pic yourself will be scarce, and definitely not enough for a full reportage. A birth photographer will set you back a few hundred dollars, pounds or euros on average. Pricey, but for that amount they'll be on call 24/7 for multiple weeks, being able to be present in the dead of night. If you can afford one, make sure to check their work and that they really have experience with birth photography. You'll want someone that knows how to stay in the background, understands that turning off shutter sounds or flashes is a must, and won't interrupt the process in any way. Should it be out of your budget, or if you just don't want to pay for it, get someone in the room that is clever enough to not get in the way and knows how to work a camera. Moms tend to love to see the photos in hindsight, especially those with a C-section. So, for whomever will be the photographer it also will be a great memory. Say ceeeeeee-section!

# WHAT YOU CAN DO



- Find a photographer with experience.
- Find a photographer whose work you like.
- Meet the photographer in advance so you can get an idea of what kind of personality you're inviting into the delivery room.
- Communicate Do's and Don'ts:
  - If there is anything you don't want captured be clear about it.
  - If there is anything you definitely want captured, be clear about it.
- Make sure to be clear on the deliverables:
  - Amount of photos or videos
  - Colour correction
  - Is video editing included?
  - Music reference for video edit
  - Delivery timeline
  - Code of conduct
- If you don't want the pictures to remain archived with the photographer, communicate this in writing.
- Communicate that if the photographer wants to use some of your photos for their portfolio that they can only do so with your permission.

# READY SET GO BAG

*Always be ready to go*



With 'go-bag', I don't mean the bag you take with you when you're 'out to get some smokes' never to return. I mean the hospital bag. You should quit smoking anyway if you haven't by now. Even if you're not planning to deliver the baby at the hospital, still make sure you have a go-bag ready, as about half of all first births planned at home end up moving to the hospital anyway because of requests for pain relief. So, make sure you have a bag ready with everything you need for your partner and baby. First baby deliveries can take between 12 and 24 hours from the first sign of a contraction, so make sure you've packed some light entertainment and comfort creators like a pregnancy pillow, a bathrobe, a salt or night lamp, for example. Your partner won't be comfortable during labour, so make sure she can be as comfortable as possible in the moments of rest in between contractions. You'd also be wise to pack an overnight bag of your own to make sure you can refresh after your bundle of joy is delivered. Bring snacks. The last thing you want is to be in the hospital cafeteria line waiting for mediocre coffee and disappointing sandwich while your offspring is brought into this world, so BYOSnacks. It's better.

# GO-BAG

## WHAT YOU CAN DO

**The go-bag**

- Birth plan.
- Bathrobe.
- Toiletries: Hairbrush, (dry) shampoo, toothbrush and paste, deodorant, hair ties, possible contacts or glasses, lip balm.
- Comfy clothes: nursing bra, joggers, hoodie, slipper socks, underwear
- Phone charger with long cord.
- Umbilical cord ring. Clamps can be uncomfortable for the baby and inconvenient for you when changing. Hospitals often only have clamps.
- Bluetooth speaker.
- Salt lamp or nightlight for a dimmed atmosphere.
- Snacks like granola bars, fruit, dextrose, or energy bars.
- Adult diapers which can be more comfortable than the pads and mesh the hospital gives your partner.
- Reusable water bottle.
- A TENS device if you plan on using it.

**Baby**

- Several bodysuits or wrap shirts, the latter are easier to use.
- Several woollen shirts in different sizes 50/56. Wool moderates body temperature in both heat and cold and is easy to clean.
- Several baby pants 50/56.
- Socks and shoes.
- Several woollen baby hats.

**Your bag**

- Camera.
- Underwear.
- Clean shirt.
- Wear layers. That way you can always take something off when it's too hot in the room and you won't be cold should you end up in an operating room. Those are cold.
- Entertainment, light reading.
- Phone charger.
- Toothbrush.
- A push present, a gift you give your partner in the delivery room or after to mark her incredible accomplishment. Generally, this results in something jewellery.
- CAR SEAT.

**Car**

- Have the car checked two months before due date.
- Drive the fastest route to the hospital so you know it.
- Prepare and stow a waterproof fabric for the car seat of the mom to be.

# DELIVERING THE BABY

*Why being an active part of the delivery is good*

In many cultures the non-birthing partner isn't welcome in the delivery room, which is a shame because their presence has been proven to be of great influence on a positive birthing experience. Also known as labour companionship, your presence in the room or that of a trusted partner plays a number of roles in supporting her during labour. It has been proven that your presence will make her feel supported, experience less pain, and feel more in control and confident, all of which will make for a positive birthing experience.[14] And that's just from being in the room, passive. When you are active in the experience and in the presence of your partner, you're also very likely to help her bridge the communication gap between her and clinical staff, provide pain relief through massage, meditation or distraction, be an advocate that speaks up in support of her preferences, and be a source of encouragement emotionally as well as physically by having her remain mobile.[15] Don't be alarmed, your presence doesn't mean you have to be at the business end of things. You can be wherever you (and she) are comfortable. Like many things in good parenting, it starts with simply showing up.

# WHAT YOU CAN DO

- Discuss her preferences to your presence in the room.
- Discuss your role in the room.
- Be an advocate for her wishes and preferences.
- Liaise between her and the clinical staff.
- Relieve her pain through massage, helping her meditate, or offering to operate the TENS device if she has one.
- Encourage her to be mobile with position suggestions: squat, hand-knees, birthstool, on her side, bath, shower, sitting.
- Encourage and reinforce her confidence with positive affirmations and breathing exercises.
- Control the mood in the room with lighting, music, or scents.

# PAIN IS BEAUTIFUL

*Your role in pain management*

This might read as a contradiction and unless you're a sadist or masochist the contradiction is generally true. However, during birth pain truly is beautiful. It's the pain of a contraction that helps your newborn out of the womb and into this world. There's much more to a birth than pain, but the basic principle of a contraction is as follows. The womb contracts and causes pain, this pain produces endorphins which helps in the anticipation of the next contraction but also helps relax the body which produces another hormone called oxytocin. Oxytocin widens the cervix making sure that the baby can move further down the birth channel with the next contraction. The next contraction produces endorphins, which produces oxytocin which widens the cervix and has the baby move further down the birth canal—a cycle that repeats itself until the baby arrives. See oxytocin as the oil that keeps the birth-engine running. And you can contribute to its production because it has been proven that light touch, kisses, loving words, hugs, cuddles, or even sex positively influence the production of the hormone. The cycle only works if the mother isn't fighting the pain but embraces it, so support her with these affectionate actions.

If she wants to use medial pain relief, there are many solutions from epidurals, Nitrous oxygen, and pethidine, to remifentanil drips. It is likely that she might have a mix of non-medical pain relief and medical pain relief throughout the delivery, in which case, help her with dosing it. For example, in the early phase give her a massage; in the active phase, operate the TENS for her; in the delivery phase she might want to use some nitrous or remifentanil, which needs to be operated by her to prevent over-dosing; and as always, you can help her with positive affirmations. Know that some medical pain relief might no longer be an option if you wait too long before using it. So, if she prefers this, make sure to learn what the best and last moments to use it are. But the first pain killing starts with you.

## WHAT YOU CAN DO

- Massage her.
- Touch or stroke her gently.
- Kiss and cuddle.
- Encourage her with loving words.
- Help her dose the different pain relief tools.
- Operate the TENS for her. TENS is an electrical nerve stimulator that you stick to her lower back that helps to relieve some of the pain of a contraction.
- Recite positive affirmations.
- Help her find her breathing rhythm.
- Discuss a safe word so your partner can truly tell you when pain becomes unbearable.

# INTERVENTIONS

*How to navigate them*

Over the last few years, hospital births have been on the rise. A side effect of this increase is that baby deliveries are being standardised, assuming every body, birth, and baby is the same. It's a system that benefits the efficiency of a hospital but not per se that of the person in labour. Several studies[16] have shown that this standardisation has led to many unnecessary 'interventions' and an American study even showed more than four out of ten women in the USA were taken into a C-section surgery because they didn't progress fast enough. These women hadn't dilated beyond 5cm, which means they weren't even in active labour yet. In other words: they might've had a good chance of delivering their baby naturally had they been given the time.

Standardising things isn't all bad. It does give us a good understanding as to how a birth unfolds and when things are going south. Any woman delivering a baby naturally will move through the latent, active, transition, delivery, and recovery phase, but everyone does that at their own pace. But you might not always get that time. Sometimes a doctor might propose an intervention to speed things up. Whatever the path to delivery you have chosen, the only reason to be rushed into a decision is because it's life threatening to mother or child. In such cases, trust the professionals with all your heart. But if it isn't life threatening, know that you have a choice and you can get council from your midwife before taking any decision. So, whenever an intervention is proposed or when you are confused about what is happening, be sure to ask questions. That is the golden rule: Keep asking. The chances that you and your partner will have a positive birth are higher when you're actively engaged. And you can be a powerful ally to your partner when she is unable to speak or think. On the right you'll find a few questions you can ask whenever there's a decision to be made.

## WHAT YOU CAN DO

- Discuss her preferences to your presence in the room.
- Whatever it is, keep asking.
- Follow the BRAIN method:
  + **Benefits** - What is the benefit of this intervention?
  + **Risk** - What is the risk of this intervention?
  + **Alternatives** - What are the alternatives?
  + **Intuition** - What does your gut tell you?
  + **Nothing** - What happens if we do nothing?
- How much time do we have until we need to make a decision?

## BASIC HUMAN BIRTH RIGHTS

Since 2010 the European Court of Human Rights decided that a woman has the right to control her birthing options, including the right to decide her care providers, birth companions, treatment options, and the circumstances of their delivery. In many places around the world this is not the case and women face abuse, obstetric violence, or PTSD. Knowing that she has these rights can give her and you more confidence in creating a positive birth experience, so double check what her rights are in the country where she will be delivering the baby.

If you and your partner feel all women should have basic human rights in childbirth regardless of where they live, you can support the cause of the HRIC with a donation.

https://humanrightsinchildbirth.org/

# EARLY LABOUR

*Something is happening*

If we are to believe Hollywood, every birth would begin with a bucket of water dropping on the floor and a woman shouting, 'I think my water just broke.' Spoiler alert. This is not how it generally goes down. It likely starts with light and irregular contractions that might be mistaken for a belly ache or period pain. They could also be very regular for some time and then suddenly disappear. In some cases, her water does break, but usually this doesn't happen until a later stage and in some cases they don't break at all unless punctured. Whatever the case, as soon as she's having regular contractions, inform the midwife and follow their instructions.

The contractions will become harder to ignore but it can still take hours, sometimes even days, before anything really happens. Although the excitement might be difficult to calm, make sure she eats and sleeps a lot. Soon the contractions are impossible to ignore and sleep will be out of the question. If the contractions last between 30 to 60 seconds and come every 3 to 4 minutes, you should definitely inform the midwife and depending on dilation and the overall situation, you're likely to start your journey to the hospital should the plan be to deliver the baby there. Until then, try to relax.

# WHAT YOU CAN DO

- Inform the midwife, doula, or any other caregiver.
- Help her relax by drawing her a bath or shower.
- Help her catch some sleep.
- Go for a walk together.
- Provide some entertainment to distract her from the pain with movies, music, or maybe MarioKart?
- Make her some light snacks because she won't be able to eat solids later.
- Catch some sleep yourself; you're going to need it.
- Time the contractions. If they last between 30 and 60 seconds and come every five minutes or less, move to the hospital if you're planning to birth there.
- Always call your midwife or doctor if anything happens before week 37.

# NO SLEEP TILL BABY

# ACTIVE LABOUR

*It is definitely happening*

It's on. Contractions are now becoming too strong to ignore, they last longer and come more frequently. They might last 60 to 90 seconds and come every 2 to 3 minutes. Hopefully, you were both able to relax a little in the early labour phase because, from now on, there's work to be done. If the plan was to go to the hospital, this is the moment to leave. (Depending on your country this might be earlier.) If you informed the midwife earlier, they're likely already there or in touch with you. But if not, this is also the moment for the midwife, doula, or other caregiver to come over. If you go to the hospital, make sure to bring the birth plan, the baby car seat, and the go-bags: hers, the baby's, and your own. Hospitals won't let you leave with your baby without a car seat, so don't forget. If you move by car, make sure to put waterproof fabric on her seat, in case her water breaks. After all driving home with your new family in a smelly car can be a stain on the magic moment.



## WHAT YOU CAN DO

- Bring the go-bags.
- Bring the baby car seat.
- Make sure hospital staff or caregivers have a copy of the birth plan.
- Help her stay hydrated by offering water and other liquids. Prevent her from eating solids because these will get in the way.
- Help her move around or change positions.
- Help her focus on the experience, not the progress, and keep her in a positive mindset.
- Make sure you eat a light snack or a dextrose tablet. No one wants to faint when the big moment happens.
- Bring a waterproof fabric or passenger seat cover.

# TRANSITION PHASE

*No turning back now*

This is the final stage of the early and active labour phase and in a relatively short time she will progress from 7 to 10 cm of dilation and her body will transition from opening the cervix to the baby's descent (though this can still last a couple of hours). She'll feel the pressure of the baby's head coming down, sometimes already with an urge to push. This is often a moment when she might feel panicky or scared as her body is taking over. This is likely a moment where you'll hear her say things like 'I can't do this'. With transition being so close to actually delivery, pain medication options will be limited, which means that if she needs relief your words and touch will be even more important. So, give her some positive encouragement. This is the phase where your words count the most, some women tend to listen well in this phase. So much even that if you tell her to calm down, breathe, or move around she will, so make your words count.

About moving around—on average 85% of women give labour on their backs and 35% of them even have their legs in stirrups.[4] Quite a high number, especially when you consider that it has been proven that a woman being free to move around and find her own ideal birthing position has considerable advantages: the delivery moves faster, the delivery takes less effort since you can use gravity, the pelvis opening is wider, the baby gets more oxygen because there is less pressure on the aorta, and there is less need for interventions or C-sections. That said, there's nothing wrong with giving birth on her back, when she's on her back it's easier for caregivers to support. But that is often also the biggest reason for having her on her back. So, when there's no need for caregiver support, have her move around.

## WHAT YOU CAN DO

- Give positive affirmations:
  + You're doing great.
  + You can do this, and you will.
  + Every contraction gets you closer to the baby.
  + You were born to do this.
  + Your body knows how to deliver; trust in your body.
  + It's not pain, it's strength.
- Motivate her to move around.
- Suggest her preferred positions, write them down below.

## NOTES

# DELIVERY PHASE

*The baby is coming*

The most exciting of phases. The baby is moving down and is slowly coming into this world. Like with many of the chapters I have written, there is much more to it than what I'm writing down, but a couple of key things to know and remember about this last stretch are the phases the baby is moving through. First, she'll reach full dilation of the cervix and get the urge to push. Know that pushing can take up to a full hour with her first child. In my partner's case, even two. First the head will come out, known as crowning (also called the ring of fire). To some, the most painful of a vaginal birth process as this is when the biggest circumference of the head is passing through. The mother is asked to pause the pushing and just breathe for a moment to prevent tearing. Once the head is fully out, there is an awkward moment where she has to pause again so they can check if the umbilical cord isn't wrapped around the head and to make sure the baby can turn its shoulders to move further out. After this, the shoulders follow and after that, the rest of the body. Most of the time they'll put the baby straight onto the chest of the mother. If they don't, make sure to remind them. Depending on your wishes the umbilical cord will be cut. Most of the time they'll wait until the umbilical cord is white. If they don't, make sure to wait because in those last few moments your baby will get much needed nutrients, blood, and oxygen from the mother. If you don't want it cut, you'll wait for the placenta expulsion and it will be packed up with the baby (also known as full lotus). Once the placenta is expelled, they'll run some tests to make sure everything went as it should. If you have special wishes about the placenta, this is also the moment to make sure it all goes to plan.

Make sure that in their first hour after birth the baby will be skin on skin with its mother, or if she's unable to, with yourself. Known as the golden hour, this has proven to help regulate the baby's temperature, helps control their respiration and lower the risk of low blood sugar, among a few things. Even if the baby can have this moment with its mother, make sure to have that moment for yourself as well, as this does a lot for the bonding with your child as well. This is where your relationship starts. Better make it a good one.

## WHAT YOU CAN DO

- Support and calm her during the ring of fire.
- Be aware of the full and half lotus, and other options.
- Make sure the umbilical cord is white before you cut it.
- Make sure that someone takes a picture when you cut the umbilical cord.
- Be aware of the placenta wishes and make sure these are honoured. You can grind them up as energy pills, supposedly feed it to the dog for bonding, make a printout of it, and many more things. You could also just dispose of it.
- Make the golden hour last as long as you can.
- Extend the golden hour with your own skin-on-skin moment.

MAKE
THEIR
GOLDEN
HOUR
SHINE

# RECOVERY PHASE

*Afterglow*

Now that your prodigy has arrived, there are still a couple of things to be done. They will examine the placenta to make sure nothing is left behind, conduct some cognitive tests on your baby and do a health check on your partner to see if any perineal damage occurred during the delivery. If there was any damage, there will be need for some sutures. If breastfeeding is on the table, this will be the moment where the midwife or hospital staff will help with some latching techniques. But for the first 24 hours, your baby will still be able to run on the nutrients they got from their mother. So, if feeding isn't working yet, don't sweat it. This phase is often a moment of relief for parents and fatigue for mom, so make sure she's able to rest. But because of the adrenaline, the fatigue might not kick in until after 24 or even 48 hours. From now on it will be important to cocoon and really connect with each other. Cocooning will not only help you bond as a family and offer your child a 'soft landing', but it also protects your child from disease over the first several weeks. You will only have this moment together once, so make sure you make the most of it. A push present might make it even more memorable. So, whip it out.



## WHAT YOU CAN DO

- Observe and participate in the health checks done to your baby.
- Make sure your wishes are followed regarding timing around the weighing, Vitamin K shots, washing, and wiping clean.
- This might be a great moment for a push present. Read the room though. If it doesn't feel right, keep it in your pocket.
- If there was a C-section, support her in every way you can and make sure she rests.
- Find as much skin-on-skin moments for you, your partner, and the baby.

# C-SECTIONS

*How to navigate them*

Natural birth isn't always so natural, and might not be possible. In which case, the baby will be delivered 'artificially' through a Caesarean, or C-section. There are many reasons why this can be the case, but generally, you can divide C-sections into two categories: planned and emergency. When there are signs that natural birth isn't in the cards a few weeks before the due date, you can plan when the baby will be delivered. Signs could be that the baby isn't in the right position, has a birth defect, the mother has a health condition, her pelvis doesn't allow vaginal birth, and sometimes if you're expecting twins. In these cases, a doctor or midwife might advise a planned C-section. When this happens, you'll have to agree on a specific date when the surgery and birth will take place. Generally, this is in week 39, but this can differ based on the state of the baby.

When your partner is in the process of giving birth naturally but runs into complications, the doctor or midwife might call for an emergency C-section. This mostly happens when the health of the mother or child is at stake. One third of all caesareans are caused by a failure to progress or a stalled labour, which means that dilation stagnates and doesn't proceed for several hours. But foetal distress, cord prolapse, or placenta issues are also reasons for a C-section. Just know that when an emergency C-section is performed that it is done to prevent further complications or damage to the health of the mother and the child. Whatever the cause of a C-section, if it occurs, learn about the possibilities for a 'gentle C-section'. A gentle C-section is designed to mimic the same birth ritual you'd have in a delivery room, but then in the operating room. The mother will be able to see the baby come out of her belly and have the same skin-on-skin and breastfeeding moment they would have in the delivery room. This makes the most of the 'golden hour' and is beneficial to both mother and child.

# WHAT YOU CAN DO

**Before and during a C-section**

- Some hospitals offer hospital tours so you can get an understanding of what to expect. Inquire with your local hospital.
- Learn about the possibilities of a gentle C-section.
- If your partner wants you to, express and represent her wishes during the procedure.
- If anything is unclear, keep asking.
- Make sure there's a chair present for you in case you feel queasy.
- Encourage and calm your partner.
- Take pictures.

**After a C-section**

- If you qualify, take paternity leave or try to work from home as much as possible. Recovery from a C-section is six weeks, so they'll need all the help you can provide.
- Make sure she rests. She needs to heal.
- She can't lift the baby, or anything else for that matter, for the first 24 to 36 hours.
- She can't drive for the first six weeks.
- Help her with getting in and out of bed.
- Organise as much skin-on-skin time for mother and child, so bring her the baby for feeding and cuddling.
- Create skin-on-skin moments with you and your baby.
- Bring pain relief, or remind her to take it timely.
- Change diapers.
- Take them to medical appointments.
- Prepare meals or ask for meal support from friends and family.
- Take on the grocery shopping, cooking. and house cleaning.

*Breastfeeding & formula*

The first few months will not be a land of milk and honey. It will solely be milk. Milk or formula is the only possible food source for you baby in the first six months, and they're not allowed to eat honey until they're one, so milk it is. When it comes to milk there are a few options, breast milk, formula, or a mixture of both. Both not meaning literally a breast and formula cocktail, but an alternation between the two.

Studies have shown that your child benefits from receiving breast milk for the first six months. However, this isn't realistic for everyone. Some might not have enough milk while others have so much the child has difficulty drinking it. Whatever the choice, formula or breastmilk, you should support your partner. Breastfeeding is hard, requires discipline, enormous energy, and becomes even harder if she goes back to work. Formula can be equally difficult because your baby might refuse the bottle, you have to carry a lot of stuff around, and the potential psychological effect it can have on your partner; and then there is this weird stigma around it. You'll find lots of opinionated people about your choice that both of you will be forced to face. Challenging as it can be, it will without a doubt be the most precious moments you'll have with your child, regardless of the milk they get. So just focus on the beauty of it.

## WHAT YOU CAN DO

- Help her with latching the baby to the breast, especially in the beginning.
- Set up a nursing station where she can feed easily.
- Set up a bottle making station where you can easily prepare the bottle without having to leave the bedroom too much.
- Buy her a breastfeeding cloth, so she can feed in privacy in public.
- Find the right bottle for your baby. This will be accomplished through trial and error: not all bottles or nipples will work for your baby.
- Once you have the one that works best, get multiples.
- Get her nipple cream in advance.
- Get her soft nipple pads.
- Get her silver nipple caps. A drop of milk on the nipple covered by a silver cap does wonders.
- Use a baby tracker app to log feeding times so you can more easily plan and time together.
- In order to prevent cramps, always try to get your baby to burp. Hold them against your shoulder and gently pat them on their backs or try the colic carry: lay them on your arm belly down and pat their backs, or massage their belly, to help them burp.

*Breastfeeding Pros & Cons*

**Breastfeeding Pros**

+ It gives the baby exactly the right nutrients the baby needs at that moment, especially if your child is born early.
+ It builds antibodies against disease.
+ It gives flexibility of movement to the mother because she can feed at any place, at any time.
+ It improves bonding between mother and child.

**Breastfeeding Cons**

- You won't exactly know how much your child actually drinks, unless you pump and have them drink from a bottle. However, a baby drinks to their needs. So, unless your child is showing signs of malnourishment, there's no need to know how much they drink.
- Breast stowage can be very painful. When the milk production is in full swing and you miss a feeding, the breast will store it to a point where it becomes so full it hurts and can even cause infection.
- Nipple fissures. If the baby doesn't latch properly, they can cause irritated, cracked, and sore nipples. Very painful. Luckily this only happens in the first few weeks.
- It puts a lot of the feeding efforts on the mother's shoulders.

*Formula Pros & Cons*

**Formula Pros**

+ You'll know exactly how much your baby drinks.
+ You can divide and conquer more easily.
+ Formula is digested slower than breastmilk, which in our case meant longer sleeps.
+ It offers easy opportunities for friends and family to feed as well.
+ Your partner can eat and drink whatever she wants

**Formula Cons**

- Formula doesn't have the exact nutrients when your baby needs it, like anti-bodies when they have a cold.
- Your baby can be allergic to formula. In which case don't worry; you can also get surrogate breastmilk from mothers who over produce.
- The feeling of not being able to feed your child with your body can have impact on your partners mental health.
- Formula can cause digestive troubles like cramps.
- It's more expensive. You'll need bottles, nipples, formula, containers, bottle heaters, and sterilisers, etc.
- It requires more work to prepare.

*How to get it*

One thing is for sure, your sleeping routine will never be the same—not necessarily in a bad way, but definitely in a different way. The sleep cycles of a newborn are different from that of an adult. Theirs last 45 to 60 minutes and they're not able to connect sleep cycles together, which means they're likely to wake up and cry. If you're lucky, they can get back to sleep on their own, but assume you'll have to help them get back to sleep. With a baby sleeping 14 to 17 hours a day in the first two to three months, this means you'll be rocking them to sleep often. Imagine your biceps, though. Each baby has their own preference as to what soothes them, but know that as soon as you find something that works, it will change faster than you think, making you have to start over again. Also, the lack of the baby's motor skills mean they often wake themselves up with a punch or scratch to the face. In which case, get a swaddle or little gloves that prevent them from doing so.

Lack of sleep can put some pressure on your relationship as well, and a way to keep both of you sane is to operate like a team and divide and conquer. If you're a night person, take the night shift and then your partner takes the morning or the other way around. This way, both know what they can expect and the burden is divided evenly. Even if your partner breastfeeds and it might feel logical to let her get up and take on the burden, support her anyway by changing the baby's diaper first before handing the little one over to your partner. Breastfeeding is hard work as it is, and being able to stay in bed for it, makes her life easier as well.

# WHAT YOU CAN DO

- Sleep whenever you can in the first few weeks. Nap when they do.
- Assume bad sleep and you'll always be delighted.
- Divide and conquer night and morning shifts.
- Get a battery-operated dimming night light so you don't wake the baby every time you change diapers or feed them.
- Get a swaddle or baby gloves. Swaddles keep them from tossing and turning or punching themselves.
- If they experience cramps, do baby bicycles: Lay them on their backs and put their knees to their chest like riding a bicycle to help them fart. Try the colic carry: lay them on your arm belly down and pat their backs, or massage their belly, to help them burp. The heat and weight of a warm bean bag on their belly also helps.
- Go to bed early.
- If you can't get any reasonable sleep, book an appointment with a sleep coach.
- If your baby doesn't sleep well, give them a bath before they go to bed. Baths work wonders.
- If you have the space, make a small diaper changing station in your bedroom so you can keep the midnight baby visits to a minimum. This is also convenient for your own sleep patterns.

# TALKING TEARS

*Communicating through crying*

We're taught that crying is a bad thing, associated with physical or emotional pain, and let's face it, P.S. I love you. When it comes to babies, crying is actually a good thing because without it we'd have no clue what to do. Since a baby's vocabulary is limited, their core way to communicate is through their tears and loud vocal cords. Each cry can be placed into four categories. They're either hungry, upset, sleepy, hurting, or all of the above at the same time. Over time you'll learn to identify which is which, but if you keep track of their feeding, pooping, and sleeping patterns, you should be able to identify more easily what is going on. So, whenever they cry, run through the scenarios. Do they need some food? Do they need a change? When did they last sleep? None of those? Perhaps a cuddle? Still crying? Maybe they have belly cramps because they just ate. If they cry longer than two hours, call a doctor. In some cases, you might have a 'cry baby' which sounds cuter than it is. In which case, good luck.

Whenever your baby cries, don't get annoyed. Instead try to interpret it as your child trying to tell you something: 'Hey, I've just eaten and gotten belly cramps, can you do some baby bicycles to help me out?' 'Yo! Old timer. I-AM-HUNGRY-FEED-ME-PLEASE.' 'Daddy-o! I left you a dookie in my diapers but it's driving me crazy. Fresh nappies please.'

# WHAT YOU CAN DO

- Keep track of your baby's feeding, pooping, and sleeping patterns.
- Remind yourself that they're trying to talk to you when they cry:
  - They're warm or cold
  - They need a new diaper
  - They're hungry
  - They have a sucking need, give them the breast or a pacifier
  - They have cramps, in which case they're likely kicking their legs
- After a breast or bottle comes a burp. If not, cramps and tears will likely follow.
- If they experience cramps, do baby bicycles: Lay them on their backs and put their knees to their chest like riding a bicycle to help them fart. Try the colic carry: lay them on your arm belly down and pat their backs, or massage their belly, to help them burp.
- Place a sleeping aid device near the bed with heartbeat sounds or white noise.
- Some music apps have womb sounds playlists. Simply play one on your phone and place it next to the bed. The heartbeat noises will remind them of their comfortable time in the womb.
- Stick to your calming ritual if your baby keeps crying and keep it going for at least ten minutes. Babies don't like change.
- Put your baby in the carrier and do some household chores; they often find it calming.
- Ensure a safe and calm environment with not too many things around the crib or playpen.
- Create routines. The more predictable a day for a baby, the better.

# DIAPER HACKING

*Tips to nail diapering*

Besides the lack of sleep, diapers tend to be another daunting feature of having a baby. And although mother nature has set it up in a clever way that slowly eases you into the world of nasty nappies, there will definitely be moments where your newborn will throw you a curveball. It will start with a weird black tar looking goo called meconium. Made of amniotic fluid, intestinal cells, enzymes, and even hairs, this is just their bodies starting up, nothing to worry about. After that, you'll next get an odourless curry-type sauce, which then slowly gain more odour, then a bit more substance, and once they start eating solids, you win the jackpot and you get it all. But by then you'll be so accustomed to it, that the stress sweats will no longer pay you a visit whenever you hear the trouser thunder. Until then, here are some things that I've learned the hard way. I can't guarantee that you'll make it out with clean hands, but they will definitely save you a handful of stress or a shirt full of pee. Let's dive into it.

## WHAT YOU CAN DO

- Embrace diaper duty as a great moment to interact with your baby. If the meconium is persistent, treat the baby's bottom with Vaseline so you can more easily wipe it off with the next diaper change.
- If you have a girl, wipe from the front to the back. If it's a boy wipe in whatever way works best.
- Always put a wipe, tissue, or pee-pee tipi on the equipment to prevent reckless spraying.

- Play the belly trumpet or say with extra jolly all the things you're doing. If you make it a playful affair, you can distract a baby from the actual business taking place and make it out without too many twists, turns, and regrets. This is mostly effective after a few weeks when they can process it better.
- If you're righthanded, lay your baby with the head to the left. If you're lefthanded, do it the other way around. And never stand at the business end or you'll risk a field goal.
- Make sure you have some sort of toy or rattle nearby so you can occupy their hands and not find them digging into their own creations.
- Peek into the diaper on the sides to see if it's number one or two. If it's one, you can always put a fresh diaper underneath their hips to make the transaction quicker. Make sure their hips are in the air so you can clean them before touching them down in their fresh diaper again. This won't win you a hygiene award, but it will save some time and tears.
- Whenever you get what my partner and I call a party diaper—a diaper that has is all, everywhere—make sure to first scoop the poop with the top part of the diaper down and fold it underneath their hips. Make sure their feet can't set foot on the changing pad or you'll risk cute, but crappy little footprints. This will save you some wipes.
- If you run into diaper rash, change diapers often, use a soft cloth with warm water, and dry gently with a hydrophilic cloth. Avoid wipes since they tend to be perfumed, which irritates the skin and makes your problem worse.
- When you wipe and want to make sure you got it all, don't lift them up by their legs or feet because this can damage their hips. Instead, lift them up from their lower back.

# BATHS

*Cleaning your baby*

The whole point of this book is to inspire dads to get their hands dirty when it comes to pregnancy, delivery, and caring for a newborn. However, it is even more important to keep your hands clean. That sounds contradictory, but the former is metaphorical and the latter literal. Babies are more at risk of infection and disease because their immune systems aren't fully developed yet. So, wash your hands more regularly than you're used to. And yes, use soap. Then there's the hygiene of the baby. Unlike when you drop a deuce, when a baby poops it won't be flushed away; rather it settles into their diaper. If you're lucky. If not, it could be everywhere, from their neck to their toes. Yes neck. You can clean up their act with copious amounts of baby wipes, but after four times on the same day, it might be time for a more thorough cleaning session; their first bath.

The first bath you'd want to do together with your partner. But after that, it can also be a great moment to relieve your partner and bond with your child. Until the umbilical cord falls off you may only want to give your baby a sponge bath. You can use baby soap for their body, though it won't be very necessary. Their face, however, should only be cleaned with water. As soon as the umbilical cord falls off you may give your baby tub baths. When you bathe them, do so in an aptly sized bath—bucket baths have been proven to help a baby relax because it reminds them of womb conditions. Regular tubs aren't recommended until they're six months old. And to be honest, when there's poop in the water, it's easier to clean a bucket. Bucket or baby baths also come with the convenience that you can do it in any room that you can heat up enough and enables you to put everything you need within arm's reach. Make sure you have everything set up before you put them in the bath. Because once they're in, you can't let them go. But trust me, you won't want to because it's way too adorable.

# WHAT YOU CAN DO

- Rule number one of baby baths: Never let a baby alone in a bath. Not even for a second.
- Rule number two of baby baths: Never let a baby alone in a bath. Not even for a second.
- Set everything up before you get them ready for a bath.
- What you'll need:
  + Clean basin or tub
  + Soft washcloth
  + Bath towels
  + Hydrophilic cloth
  + Diaper
  + Outfit
  + Comb or brush
  + Baby soap and shampoo but try to keep it to a minimum because it can make their skin dry
  + Baby oil or lotion
- Make sure the water isn't warmer than 38°C or 100°F; use a thermometer.
- Make sure the room is warm and draft free; baby's get cold fast.
- Don't bathe them more than three days a week; more can dry out their skin.
- Only give them a sponge bath until the umbilical cord falls off.
- Make sure to have a camera within arm's reach.
- Pat them to dry, don't wipe, and make sure the towel is soft.

# CLOTHING

*They really do grow faster than you think*

With an average growth of 4.4cm in the first month alone, your baby's wardrobe will shrink faster than you think. You can prepare for this by getting multiple sizes in advance because, although doctors and midwives can pretty accurately predict the size of your newborn, they never tell you how this translates into clothing size and there's always some variability between their predicted size and their actual size.

The length of the baby generally directly translates to the size chart; a baby of 50cm tall will perfectly fit a 50-52 romper. But you won't have their official size until they're actually born and babies don't grow linearly. That 4.4cm growth in the first month might actually happen in one day. They don't neatly grow 15mm per day. One day that sweater fits like a glove, and the next it looks like a crop top. So, when you're out prepping to stock the wardrobe of your newborn, make sure to buy a couple of different sizes. Also pay attention to how a specific item is put on. For example, Kimono-style or side-snap bodysuits are far easier than bodysuits that go over the head. Make sure you don't get anything with zippers or buttons on the back because this can be uncomfortable for the baby, and will be uncomfortable for you when you have to change them. The right wardrobe can be the difference between sweet smiles or bitter tears for both the baby and you. So, shop wisely.

# WHAT YOU CAN DO

- Buy different sizes in advance.
- Always buy one size too big.
- Get side-snap bodysuits instead of bodysuits that go over the head. This will make for smoother diaper changes.
- Get bodysuits with adjustable crotch buttons for a better fit and longer use.
- Make sure none of the buttons or zippers are on the back. This will make for smoother diaper changes and fewer tears.
- Take seasons into consideration when buying. They might not fight that awesome Gundam snow suit by the time it's winter.
- Ask family for bigger sizes if they want to gift clothing.
- Get a drool bib or bandana, especially when teething. The amount of drool they produce easily soaks their whole outfit.
- In the first few months, woollen clothing is very practical. It insulates, keeps dry, and makes for easy dressing due to its stretch.
- Always dress one layer warmer than you would yourself. Especially in the beginning, babies can't regulate their own heat yet, so make sure they're warm.

# BABY BLUES

*When cloud nine is a thundercloud*

Your bundle of joy doesn't always come with an overload of happiness. In some cases that cloud nine comes with more thunder that you initially expected. In fact, about one in ten women experience symptoms of postpartum depression,[17] [18] which can be as severe and serious as full-blown depression. For most women it won't be as serious, but the occurrence of that cloud nine happiness is about as rare. Baby blues are very common; most parents experience these feelings for the first few weeks. Generally, they start around day two or three and can last up to two weeks. The hormonal change after birth combined with recovery, parenting anxiety, a crying baby, and breastfeeding pressures can weigh heavily on the emotions. On both of your emotions, by the way. So don't be surprised when either of you feels cranky, sad, lonely, or indecisive or has trouble sleeping. Like most blues, after a while they'll evaporate like snow in the sun. If they don't disappear, something more serious might be happening and you might need some support. Both new mothers and partners[19] can experience postpartum depression, so keep an eye out for each other, and if you're in doubt, call for help.

## WHAT YOU CAN DO

- Call a health provider when:
  + The blues haven't disappeared after two weeks
  + You notice the blues are becoming worse
  + You or your partner have thoughts of harming yourself or your baby.
  + The blues make it hard for you or your partner to care for your baby.
  + The blues make it hard for you or your partner to do everyday chores.
- Sleep as much as possible and help her to sleep as much as possible.
- Enable moments alone for her and for yourself.
- Try to connect with other new parents.
- Don't drink or use drugs.
- Exercise. It will help reduce stress and give you energy.
- Eat healthily.

# BOND FROM THE BEGIN NING

*Connecting with your baby*

As stated earlier, moms have an advantage when it comes to bonding with your child. So, once the baby is born it's important to get as many skin-on-skin moments as you can with your newborn, especially in the first few months. This is known as kangaroo care.[20] This practice has been proven to increase the health of the baby, especially premature ones, increases bonding with the parents, benefit breastfeeding, reduce symptoms of postpartum depressions, and even benefit the baby's social skills later in life.[21] If your baby is delivered by C-section, this bonding is even more important for a non-birthing partner because it will stabilise the baby's heart rate and body temperature, make them cry less, and start their feeding behaviour earlier. It's also beneficial to you; studies have shown that non-birthing partners who took on Kangaroo care after a C-section suffered less from anxiety and depression and had better role attainment.[22] So, take off that shirt whenever you can and kickback with your naked baby on your chest.

## WHAT YOU CAN DO

- Create skin-on-skin moments after delivery.
- Take on skin-on-skin kangaroo care after a C-section.
- Sing a song—any song. If you want to bust out Ice Cube's 'It Was a Good Day', do it, in womb and out of womb.
- Cuddle, touch and stroke either of them whenever you can.
- Carry your baby around in a baby carrier.
- Read the little one books.
- Talk to them.

# FIRST DAMAGE

*The first time your kid gets hurt*

Even the most careful parent will eventually find their kid in harm's way. A nosedive off the couch, a clumsy bump to the head, or their slapping themselves in the face with a spoon—there is no way that you'll be able to protect your child from all the bumps and bruises of life. It's the cost of learning for both the baby and for yourself. You might be able to fend it off for a while, but sooner or later your kid will take some damage and I can assure you, your heart will be in your throat when they do. Their pain will be yours. Children are curious by nature but lack the experience to gauge the risk of their curiosity and often times miss the reflexes to fend off even the simplest of dangers like a swinging door. This is partly the reason why every day nearly two thousand children die as a result of a preventable injury.[23] Five of the most common unintentional injuries reported by the World Health Organization are road traffic injuries, falls, burns, drowning, and poisoning. So being vigilant and careful is good; being prepared for it is even better.

## WHAT YOU CAN DO

- Take a first-aid course for infants and children.
- Never leave a baby unattended in high places, for example the dresser, couch, or bed.
- Use the appropriate rail height in their crib.
- Install an aero-sleep in between the sheet cover and the mattress; should the baby sleep on its belly they will still be able to breathe. (Make sure to check whether you can use an Aero-sleep product. Some shouldn't be used early on because they can interfere with your baby's nascent ability to regulate its own temperature.)
- Don't put any objects in the baby's crib.

- Install power socket covers on all sockets.
- Install baby gates near stairs.
- Never leave a baby unsupervised in the bathtub.

**House**

- Lower the heat on your central heating to below 50C.
- Keep the bathroom secured at all times.
- Remove hazards like sharp or pointy elements from your interior.
- Put locks on cabinets that hold chemicals such as dishwasher or laundry detergent pods, cleaning agents, industrial chemicals, or medications. Magnetic locks are very convenient for you and safe for your child.
- Keep window blind cords out of reach or replace them with cordless blinds.[24]
- To eliminate choking hazards, test small objects using a toilet paper tube: if the object fits it is too small.
- Create a safe zone for a baby to play during chores, perhaps with a play fence.
- Keep windows guarded.
- Skip tablecloths.
- Don't hold hot beverages while carrying your child and keep them out of reach when on the table.

**Pets**

- Never leave a child alone with a dog or cat, no matter how friendly.
- Don't let your cat in the baby room. Cats can form a choking risk by sitting on their faces.
- Never let your child pet a dog without asking its owner.
- Don't let your child play aggressive games with a dog, like tug-of-war or wrestling.

# FIRST AID OVERVIEW

*Be prepared. Book a first aid course.*

## 1 SAFETY

Make sure you can provide first aid safely.

## 2 ASSESS

Assess the child, check if it is conscious and breathing. Try to understand what is wrong.

## 3 ALARM

If the child isn't conscious or has trouble breathing call emergency services. In doubt? Call.

## 4 ACT

Provide help. Check the airways. Secure breathing.

# FIRST AID OVERVIEW

*Be prepared. Book a first aid course.*

A

## AIRWAY

Make sure the airway is clear.

B

## BREATHING

Once the airway is clear, confirm breathing. If necessary, provide rescue breathing.

C

## CIRCULATION

If the child isn't breathing, go straight to chest compressions and rescue breathing.[25]

# SHARED PAIN IS HALF THE PAIN

# DIVIDE AND CONQUER

*Team work makes the days work.*

A few weeks after your baby is born you'll find people asking you about whether or not you have found your rhythm yet. They're not talking about your dance floor moves but about the flow you and your partner have gotten into with the baby. You won't be needing your dance floor moves for a while. The only way to find that rhythm is by operating as a team and to work with each other's strengths. Are you the better chef? You pick up the cooking while your partner cares for the baby. If you walk the dog late at night, you might as well look after the midnight feeding so your partner can sleep longer. It's not rocket science, but it does require communication and an open attitude—something that is easier said than done on little sleep.

## WHAT YOU CAN DO

- Avoid the blame game. You're both learning and messing up. Use it as a learning moment for both rather than a blaming moment for one.
- Discuss and plan the ideal rhythm for both of you and the baby.
- Make a care schedule. If your baby goes to day care, decide who brings them in and who picks them up. If one works full time, have that parent put your kid to bed, for example.
- If there are any work-related issues during the week, announce it up front so you can both prepare for it.
- Keep track of the baby's feeding, sleeping, and chasing times in a baby tracker app so both of you knows what's up at any time.
- Agree to both communicate whenever either of you needs a breather. If you give each other space to step out of the baby bubble every now and then, you can provide some relief for each other when it matters.
- If you notice she's having a rough time or a bad day, pro-actively alleviate some of the care duties.

# BEHOLDING THE BABY

*The schedule of visiting*

Babies are magnetic. Family you haven't seen in years are suddenly drawn to your doorstep. But your aunt's entitled attitude doesn't trump the recovery of mother and child. It is up to you and your partner to decide who can visit and when. If you want to be efficient, host a maternity visit party in which you hit all birds with one stone, get the whole fam together to inspect your newborn, and be done with it. Pace it slowly with one visit every week, or have the grandparents visit in the delivery room. Whatever the case, make sure you clearly communicate it and set the right expectations up front so there are no unwelcome surprises or relatives. When you send out the birth cards add the maternity visit plan, make sure they reach out to you to plan a visit and as a last resort, switch off your doorbell. After all, why would you open the door if there's no one to open it to.

## WHAT YOU CAN DO

- Be the central point of contact to plan maternity visits.
- Add the maternity visit plan to the birth card but understand that whomever you send a card will see it as an invite. So maybe think twice about the ones you'd rather not see.
- Buy maternity snacks and drinks for your guests in bulk so you only have to get it once.
- Manage visiting time. Tell visitors they're welcome for one hour as to not wear out your partner and baby. With the risk of coming across rude, remind people to leave after an hour to protect her recovery.
- If visitors ask how they can help, ask them to bring a homecooked meal. You won't have the energy to prepare them yourself those first weeks, and you can get take-out only so much without your arteries clogging up. So, take them up on their offer.
- Don't plan more visits than two a day: one in the morning and one in the afternoon.
- Make sure every visitor washes their hands, even if they won't hold the baby.
- Keep ill people away from your baby: people with a cold, the flu, cold sores, or shingles.

EVERY PARENT STARTS AS AN AMATEUR

# WELL BABY VISIT

*Preventative paediatric care check-ups*

I don't know if there is such a thing as being ready for a baby. There comes a point where it either just happens, or where mother nature's biological clock kind of forces you to go for it should you ever want children. The reason I say this is because the first moment you're alone with your child you realise how unprepared and unskilled you actually are. Even after nine months of preparing I felt it was immensely irresponsible of the hospital to leave the baby in our amateur, panicky parent care. But fear not. Soon enough there will be a health and wellness check up by a paediatrician or nurse to make sure your baby is doing fine and when you will get confirmation about your parenting competence. If you're confident in your own parenting skills, you should know that preventative paediatric care isn't obliged. However, getting a pair of objective eyes on your baby's health never hurts and even the most confident parent can always improve. If you decide to engage in these well baby visits, know that it isn't always covered by your insurance so make sure to double check your health care. Then again, you can't put a number to the health of your baby.

## WHAT YOU CAN DO

- Visit at 2 weeks, 2 months, 4 months, 6 months, 9 months, 12 months, 15 months, 18 months, 2 years, 2 1/2 years, 3 years, 4 years, 5 years.
- Check the location of the paediatrician's office, you might go often in the beginning and the closer you are the easier it is to visit.
- Check in with friends and families about paediatricians to consider.
- Check the credentials of the paediatrician.
- Check if your insurance covers the preventative care.

*Getting back on the horse*

Happy news travels fast, which means you'll soon hear phrases like 'say goodbye to your sex life' and although it will definitely change, not all is lost. In fact, in the second trimester your partner's libido can sky-rocket and women who've never experienced an orgasm before could climax for the first time (no offence to your bedroom skills). Some women even climax during labour.[26] So there is definitely room for some fun. Unless a doctor or midwife has clearly instructed you not to have sex, it can be business as usual. Your child will be safe. So, no worries about bumping it on the head. But you might want to try out some new baby belly-proof positions.

After birth things will be sore and it can take some time before she feels comfortable and confident enough to get back on the horse. This can be weeks, but sometimes months. Not strange if you think about the recovery that needs to happen to the body, mind, and hormones. A birth is, in a way, a trauma to the body and this needs to heal physically, but also hormonally. After birth, her prolactin levels increase, her oestrogen levels plummet and her libido likely with it. If she got an oxytocin drip during labour or is breastfeeding, the flow of oxytocin might already satisfy her need to be intimate. This is also nature's way to make sure the healing process isn't disturbed. There might also be some insecurities that creep in after you've seen her give birth.

Besides hers, your hormones also change; in order to keep you from seeking sexual refuge elsewhere and to make sure to bond with the chid, mother nature makes your testosterone levels take a dip too. Add to this the overall fatigue you'll both experience in the first few weeks and you can imagine it can take some time. However long it takes, listen to her and her body. Breastfeeding can make her vagina dryer, so be gentle, bring lube and give foreplay the proper time. It is like riding a bike, if you haven't cycled for a while, you don't just jump on and ride at top speed right out of the gate. You take it slow to get used to the pedals again.

## WHAT YOU CAN DO

- Listen to her and her body.
- Talk about it; if she's not ready understand how you can support.
- Don't guilt trip her into it.
- Help her feel sexy again. She's been puked, pooped, and peed on and is likely a feeding factory. She might not feel her most sexy self. Give her compliments, cuddles, and affection.
- Take it easy when you get back to it.
- Make it fun and light-hearted when you get back to it, take off the pressure. The more comfortable you both are the easier it is to find a rhythm again.
- Masturbate. Maybe even together.
- If she is still pregnant, try out different belly-proof positions.
- Agree to making time for intimacy together on a (bi)daily bases. This doesn't have to include sex.
- Wear protection. A woman that gave birth might be ovulating before she gets her period. So especially in those first weeks, wear protection
- Get some lubricant. Sex after a birth sometimes needs some help.

# BACK TO WORK

*Working with a baby*

If a baby isn't hard work on its own, wait until you're both back to actual work. Even though emancipation has done a lot for modern society, it still hasn't gotten to a point where you both start work at the same time in many places, unfortunately. So, you're likely to have already adjusted to the working life when your partner hasn't even started yet. Use your comfort with being a parent and a professional to support your partner, because getting back to work when you've given birth and might still be breastfeeding can be very demanding. Dropping your baby off at day care and leaving the baby in the care of someone else so you can go to work, can be equally difficult. So, team up, communicate, plan ahead, and divide and conquer. Together you can make work work out for the both of you.

# WHAT YOU CAN DO

- Plan your shared working schedule.
- Plan ahead during the week.
- Figure out a morning routine that sets whoever drops your baby off.
- Divide drop off and pick up at day care.
- Make sure to communicate preferences to your day care if anything happens that you don't like right away so you don't have to sweat it during the day.
- Discuss flexible work hours at work so you can pick up your child.
- When you pick a day care, make sure they have a parent portal or app so you both can stay updated on their day and plan accordingly.
- If your day care has a parent portal, make sure you have installed the app before you go to work.
- Align day care with your work schedules and baby sleep schedules so you can plan for some time together at the end of the day.
- Switch off when you're home with your baby. If you do need to pick up some work, do it after they've gone to bed.
- If your partner uses a breast pump, make sure to align with her as to who takes out deep frozen milk and makes sure it is brought to day care with your baby.

# ON THE ROAD

*Leaving the comfort of your home*

Some people won't even open their drapes for weeks once their bundle of joy has arrived. Others like myself, are out and about in the first few days. There is no truth about what is right and wrong when it comes to going about, as long as you make sure they're comfortable and warm. Even if you're planning to cocoon[27] for the first month, there will be a moment when you can no longer hide yourselves from the world. And when you finally go out, you'll find a whole new world—a world of forgotten rompers after an explosive diaper, shopping mall crying marathons, and misplaced pacifiers. In the beginning, your partner might not be as mobile as you remembered her to be, which means you'll be in charge of carrying your offspring around, and likely that you'll be packing the bag a lot. It will be tempting to think at some point, 'we'll only be a little while, let's leave all that crap at home'. But there's is this weird sort of laziness-karma that delivers a hungry baby, explosive diaper, or projectile vomit to you whenever you do this. So on the next page you'll find some rules to live by when you go out.

## WHAT YOU CAN DO

- Expect the worst. And pack accordingly.
- Formula: bring hot water in a thermos, cold water, and pre-dose the formula in a dispenser..
- Breastfeeding: breastfeed cloth, hydrophilic cloth.
- Diapers, Change mat, wipes, clean romper, pants, and shirt.
- Bring an extra shirt for yourself should you have to deal with projectile vomit or poop.
- Pacifier (on a cord so it can't be tossed away).
- Small toy.
- Sunhat/winter hat.
- Sunscreen for babies.
- If you go for a day or longer, bring a baby travel cot. There are nice foldable ones that weigh next to nothing and don't take much space.

# FIRST HOLIDAY

*Where to go when the walls are closing in*

Whereas before you'd plan your holidays based on destinations, flights, travel times, or apartment location, you'll now have to do it from the perspective of a parent, which can be intimidating. Flights, apartment, food, temperature, traffic, or nature are all things that can cause potential breakdowns.

The success to any baby trip is to not have any expectations. Think of it like being at home, but in another country. Expect to see nothing except the things you can see from the hotel, apartment, or cabin window. Everything else that you get to see or do is a win. A baby flying without tears or sleeping for the entire drive is the dream, but you can't plan on that. So, in order to not have any disappointment, expect nothing. Or better yet, expect the worse. That will ease a lot of the pressure and stress and will make for a great trip. Don't worry, there will be plenty of down moments when you can enjoy your trip, but in order to make sure you get the most out of it, a few pointers on the next page.

# WHAT YOU CAN DO

- Get your baby a passport.
- Travel as light as you can.
- Get a small, lightweight, foldable, and cheap stroller that can get damaged.
- Buy diapers on location.
- Bring extra clothes. They will vomit. They will poop.
- Book accommodations with baby equipment to reduce luggage. Think baby bed, chair, books, or toys.
- Book accommodations without stairs, with elevators, and with separate sleeping rooms and avoid noisy areas.
- Book accommodations with in-house laundry facilities or with laundry service nearby.
- If you fly, aim to feed the baby during take-off and landing. Babies can't clear their ear pressure voluntarily and swallowing or sucking helps to clear their ears.
- Rent a car with car seat if you can. Taxies are unlikely to have them. Or book a place close to public transport stations so you can easily get in and out.
- Bring a carrier.
- Don't be afraid to call off activities if they aren't working out.
- If you fly, get everything out of the stroller and into a bag before customs.
- Bring a white noise device or use your phone. Your baby will have to get used to the new place and need all the comforting they can get.
- Avoid planning a trip during a developmental leap.
- Flying far? Stay long. Baby jetlag is a thing and can last three days. And when they wake up at 03:00 thinking it's morning there isn't much you can do.
- Plan on doing less than you're used to on holiday.

# SELF-CARE

*How to stay sane*

Becoming a parent doesn't mean you'll completely lose your own identity. The things you loved doing before you became a dad likely won't change and it's important to fuel those passions. However, it will be hard to flex your street cred when you have a drooling baby strapped to your chest. So, the one thing you will lose is your sense of shame. But other than that, most things will stay the same. If you'd love to skate, run, game, cycle, drink, paint, or skydive before the baby, you'll like those after. You might however think twice about the risks you take.

The freedom that you had before where you could chase those passions at whatever time suited you is gone. Forget those after work drinks turning into an all-night karaoke bender. However, you can plan all-night karaoke benders in advance, and you should. Every parent needs these moments to recharge, and I think they're key in making you a great parent. Doing the things you love makes you happy, and a happy parent makes happy kids. You'll have more patience and energy and will be more resilient. That goes for both you and your partner, so make sure to plan for some happiness together.

# WHAT YOU CAN DO

- Schedule self-care moments for both of you.
- If she needs a moment for herself, prevent yourself from bothering her at those moments.
- Communicate clearly if an unexpected moment arises for some fun.
- Try to be predictable in self-care moments so you can both plan around it.
- Plan day dates with friends or fellow dads because it is more difficult to leave the house in the evenings.
- Make sleep a priority.
- Exercise. Covid taught us a workout can easily happen in your living room.

# NO ONE IS AN ISLAND

# INFINITE GRATITUDE

Coming up with an idea for a book is one thing, seeing it through to have it published is another. I wrote and designed this book over the course of months, from a few weeks before my son was born to his first birthday, while starting a new job. As such, there were many moments of doubt, stress, and anxiety that I couldn't have written through if it weren't for my intelligent, beautiful, funny, and above all motivating wife Amé. Her suggestions, sounding board, insights, and efforts to help me write while having a newborn have made all the difference. You are my partner in creativity, parenting, and the love of my life.

The trust and support of my publisher BIS, or specifically Bionda Dias, has made the difference of this book being a private list of tips sitting in a notes document on my phone or the hardcopy book it is today.

The knowledge and validation of midwives Doriët Roeleveld-van Gaalen and Maxime Welie have taught me a thing or two and most importantly made sure the book truly helps and doesn't harm. John Loughlin's linguistic expertise made sure this book wasn't confusing, actually readable, and grammatically correct, for which I can't thank him enough.

Last but not least, I want to thank the inspiration of this book, my son Jae. You just started saying mama and dada so you can't read just yet. But I can't wait to hopefully see you read this book one day. This one is for you.

# SOURCES & REFERENCES

This book is a collection of facts, viewpoints, and experiences. Most of the tips came directly from personal experience, family, friends, and the knowledge of midwives Doriët van Gaalen-Roeleveld and Maxime Welie. The rest comes from books, scientific research papers, and news outlets. I've tried to bring as much research and statistics into the book as I could. Yet with a pregnancy being heavily influenced by local culture I haven't always been able to find universal statistics that ring true in every home across the world. The World Health Organisation has conducted a lot of research in this field but not always as specific as I needed it to be. So, in some cases there might be a slight deviation in numbers when it comes to your country.

## REFERENCES


1. De eerste duizend dagen, het fundamentele belang van een goed begin vanuit biologisch, medisch en maatschappelijk perspectief, Tessa Roseboom, april 2018, Uitgeverij de tijdstroom.
2. Effects of Prenatal Exposure to the Dutch Famine on Adult Disease in Later Life: An Overview, Tessa J Roseboom, Jan van der Meulen, Anita C.J. Ravelli, November 2001, Twin Research 4(5):293-8, DOI:10.1375/1369052012605.
3. A Healthier Future by Investing in the best Start in Life, Tessa Roseboom, April 2016, TEDxAUCollege.
4. The Positive Birth Book, Milli Hill, March 2017, Pinter & Martin Ltd.
5. What If? Serious Scientific Answers to Absurd Hypothetical Questions, Randall Munroe, September 2015. John Murray Press.
6. Role of Maternal Age and Pregnancy History in Risk of Miscarriage: Prospective Register-based Study, 20 March 2019 BMJ 2019; 364 doi: https://doi.org/10.1136/bmj.l869.
7. Miscarriage: worldwide reform of care is needed, The Lancet, April 26, 2021, DOI:https://doi.org/10.1016/S0140-6736(21)00954-5.
8. Why we need to talk about losing a baby, M.Purdie, WHO. https://www.who.int/news-room/spotlight/why-we-need-to-talk- about-losing-a-baby.